THE TRUE STORY OF JELLY ROLL, THE MUSICIAN WHO STRUGGLED WITH ADDICTION AND WON HEARTS

THE JOURNEY OF A MAN WHO FOUGHT TOUGH BATTLES AND MADE PEOPLE SMILE

BY

GRACELYN WILSON

DISCLAIMER

Please note that the information in this document is provided for informational purposes only. Every effort has been made to present accurate, current, reliable, and complete information. However, no guarantees of any kind are stated or implied. Readers acknowledge that the content of this book is derived from various sources. By reading this document, the reader agrees that the author is not liable, under any circumstances, for any direct or indirect losses arising from the use of the information provided, including but not limited to errors, omissions, or inaccuracies.

TABLE OF CONTENT

Early Life and Beginnings

A look into his childhood in Nashville

Jelly Roll's story began in Nashville, Tennessee, a city known for its vibrant music scene, where country legends and up and coming artists alike have walked the streets, guitars slung over their shoulders. But for young Jason Bradley DeFord, better known today as Jelly Roll, the city represented something entirely different during his childhood. Born on December 4, 1984, his early years were shaped by a complex mix of hardships, challenges, and an environment far removed from the glitzy lights of Nashville's famed music stages.

Growing up in a lower-income neighborhood, Jelly Roll faced many of the struggles common to families living in disadvantaged communities. His family wasn't wealthy, and the instability of his home life deeply affected his worldview as a child. This was a world where opportunities seemed scarce, and difficulties loomed large. As a boy, he watched as friends and peers drifted into troubling paths, caught in the web of crime and addiction that often plagued the area.

School was not a refuge for him, either. He struggled academically and socially, never quite fitting in. His behavior often led him into trouble, and as he got older, those early signs of rebellion became more pronounced. Music, however, was one of the few constants in his life. Nashville's deep-rooted love for country music was in the air, but Jason was drawn to the raw energy and emotion of hip-hop. The beats, the lyrics, and the gritty reality of the music resonated with him in a way that nothing else did at the time. It became his escape, a way to express himself when words failed in other areas of his life.

His first steps into music
Jelly Roll's first steps into music were more of a necessity than a deliberate career choice. In the chaos of his teenage years, when he found himself entangled in trouble and struggling with the consequences of bad decisions, music became his lifeline. The legal troubles that began to pile up made him feel even more isolated,

and it was during these tough times that he realized music could offer him something he hadn't found anywhere else a voice, a sense of purpose, and an outlet for his frustrations.

He began to experiment with lyrics, using rap as a way to tell his story. His early songs were deeply personal, reflecting the rough edges of his life. These weren't polished tracks designed for mass appeal; they were raw, honest, and filled with the kind of grit that came from living through real struggles. In local circles, he started to gain attention, not just for his talent but for the authenticity he brought to his music. He wasn't just making music for the sake of it, he was telling his story, and people were listening.

Performing at small venues around Nashville, Jelly Roll started to build a local following. These early performances were often in less-than-glamorous settings, but they offered him the chance to refine his style and connect with audiences who related to his message. The underground hip-hop scene in Nashville, though smaller compared to larger cities, was a tight-knit community, and Jelly Roll quickly found his place in it. He collaborated with local artists, releasing mixtapes and singles that slowly began to spread beyond the city.

His breakthrough came when he teamed up with another Nashville rapper, Lil Wyte. Their collaboration on the song "Pop Another Pill" caught fire, gaining millions of views online and establishing Jelly Roll as more than just a local artist. This success gave him a taste of what was possible and pushed him further into the world of music. What began as an emotional outlet during hard times was quickly evolving into something much bigger, ula career that would soon take him places he hadn't even imagined.

Battling Addiction and Dark Days

His struggles with addiction

Jelly Roll's struggles with addiction are central to his story, shaping both his personal life and his music. His battle with drugs and alcohol began at a young age, fueled by the chaotic environment he grew up in. Addiction became a way to numb the pain and escape the harsh realities of life in Nashville's tough neighborhoods. Like so many around him, he fell into a cycle of substance abuse, seeking relief from the emotional turmoil that seemed to surround him.

As a teenager, his legal troubles often stemmed from his involvement with drugs. Arrests and court appearances became a regular part of his life, each one pulling him deeper into the struggle. By the time he was in his early twenties, addiction had a firm grip on him, making it increasingly difficult to envision a future where he could break free from its hold. His music, during this time, reflected the darkness he was experiencing. While he had begun to build a name for himself in the underground hip-hop scene, his personal life was spiraling out of control.

There were moments when he tried to fight back, to regain control over his life, but the pull of addiction was strong. For Jelly Roll, addiction wasn't just about the substances it was tied to his deeper emotional wounds. The traumas of his past, his sense of isolation, and the pressure of living a life filled with conflict all contributed to the cycle. He often found himself at rock bottom, trapped between his desire to overcome his addiction and the reality of how deeply entrenched it had become.

Music became his saving grace, the one thing that could pull him back from the edge. Through his lyrics, he poured out his pain and struggles, creating songs that reflected his battle with addiction. His fans, many of whom faced similar issues, connected deeply with his honesty and vulnerability. Jelly Roll's openness about his addiction was rare in a genre that often glorifies excess, and it became a defining characteristic of his work.

How addiction impacted his personal life and career

Addiction left a deep imprint on both Jelly Roll's personal life and his burgeoning career, creating obstacles that he would struggle to overcome for many years. In his personal life, addiction strained his relationships with family and friends, isolating him from those who cared about him most. His reliance on drugs and alcohol became a barrier, preventing him from fully connecting with the people around him. He often found himself stuck in a cycle of self-destruction, where addiction not only fed into his emotional pain but also kept him from healing. The toll was heavy, and for a time, it seemed that his relationships with loved ones would be irreparably damaged.

As his addiction deepened, so did the legal consequences that followed him. Repeated run-ins with the law, arrests, and court dates kept pulling him away from any sense of stability. He spent time in and out of jail, and with each arrest, his future seemed more uncertain. The personal chaos he experienced because of addiction overshadowed any success he was beginning to build in his musical career. It became harder for him to focus on his craft, and the unpredictability of his life made it difficult to sustain any momentum. There were times when addiction made it feel as though his career might never take off, as if the darkness he was living in would keep him from reaching his full potential.

His music, though, was one area where the impact of addiction was both destructive and strangely productive. On one hand, addiction slowed his progress, making it difficult to stay consistent with his output and undermining opportunities to perform or promote his work. On the other hand, it gave him a deep well of emotion and experience to draw from in his songwriting. His fans related to the pain and the raw honesty that filled his lyrics, and his struggles with addiction became part of the reason people connected so deeply with his music.

Despite the hardships, Jelly Roll's ability to turn his personal demons into art kept him moving forward. The emotional depth that addiction brought to his music helped set him apart in the underground scene, but it also meant that he was constantly battling to keep his career on track. Every step forward seemed to come with setbacks. Missed opportunities, erratic behavior, and the weight of addiction kept him from reaching the heights he knew he was capable of.

Yet, through all of this, Jelly Roll's perseverance became a defining feature of his career. His willingness to be open about his struggles, even when addiction was threatening to derail everything, gave him a unique voice in the world of music. Over time, as he worked toward recovery, he began to regain control of both his life and career, setting the stage for the success that would come once he had finally broken free from the grip of addiction. The scars of those years remain, but they also became a source of strength for him, fueling the music that would carry him forward.

Redemption and the Turning Point

How he overcame addiction

Jelly Roll's journey to overcoming addiction was not a straight path; it was filled with setbacks, moments of despair, and the constant temptation to give up. But at the heart of his recovery was a deep realization that his life needed to change, that he had reached a point where continuing down the same path would only lead to destruction. His decision to fight back against addiction came after years of struggling, facing legal troubles, and losing close relationships. He knew that if he didn't make a change, he would lose everything.

One of the first steps in his recovery was acknowledging that he couldn't do it alone. For years, he had tried to manage his addiction on his own terms, believing he could control it without outside help. But as the consequences of his actions continued to mount, he realized that professional support and guidance were necessary. This understanding led him to seek treatment and enter a recovery program, where he began the difficult process of facing the root causes of his addiction.

In treatment, Jelly Roll was confronted with the emotional and psychological wounds that had fueled his substance abuse for so long. It wasn't just about the drugs or alcohol; it was about the pain he had been carrying for years the feelings of failure, loss, and abandonment that had driven him to seek comfort in addiction. Through counseling and therapy, he began to peel back the layers of his trauma, allowing himself to heal and move forward. This process wasn't easy, and there were times when he questioned whether he could truly stay sober. But each time, he found the strength to keep going, often drawing on the support of those around him and his deep desire to rebuild his life.

Music played a pivotal role in his recovery as well. It had always been a source of expression for him, but during this time, it became a tool for healing. Writing songs allowed him to channel his emotions and confront his demons in a way that felt cathartic. He turned to music not only as a means of processing his struggles but also as a way to inspire others. His lyrics, filled with honesty about his addiction and the battle to overcome it, resonated with fans who were going through their own challenges. Knowing that his music could help others gave him an added sense of purpose and motivated him to stay on the path of recovery.

Along the way, Jelly Roll surrounded himself with people who supported his sobriety friends, family, and fellow musicians who understood what he was going through and offered encouragement. These relationships became a crucial part of his recovery, helping him stay grounded and focused on his goals. Slowly, he began to rebuild his life, taking things one day at a time. He made amends with the people he had hurt, reconnected with loved ones, and worked tirelessly to repair the damage that addiction had caused in both his personal life and his career.

Key moments that inspired his recovery
A moment came when Jelly Roll hit rock bottom emotionally. After years of pushing people away and isolating himself, he found himself in a place of

profound loneliness. His relationships had suffered he was disconnected from family and friends, and the support network that could have helped him had been fractured by his actions. It was during these moments of isolation that he began to reflect deeply on the choices he had made. The emptiness he felt in those moments helped him realize that if he didn't seek help, he would continue to spiral, perhaps to a point where there was no return. This moment of reflection marked a turning point, pushing him to reach out for the support he had long resisted.

In addition to his personal reflections, the birth of his daughter played a pivotal role in his recovery. Becoming a father added a new sense of responsibility to his life, giving him a reason to fight harder against his addiction. The desire to be present for his daughter, to provide her with a stable and loving father, was a driving force in his decision to get sober. He knew that he couldn't be the father he wanted to be while caught in the cycle of addiction. The thought of missing out on her life, or being unable to provide her with the guidance and support she would need, was a powerful wake-up call.

Jelly Roll also found inspiration through the support of his fans. As his music began to gain traction, he received messages from people who connected deeply with the raw honesty of his lyrics. Fans shared their own stories of addiction, struggle, and recovery, and their words of encouragement reminded him that he wasn't alone in his battle. Knowing that his music could help others made him realize that he had a responsibility not just to himself, but to the people who looked up to him. This realization that his story could inspire others to seek help became a source of strength, fueling his determination to stay sober.

Lastly, the fear of losing his health was another major turning point. After years of substance abuse, his body was beginning to show the physical toll of addiction. He knew that if he continued, his health would deteriorate further, potentially leading to irreversible consequences. This fear, combined with the desire to be present for his daughter and to continue pursuing his music, pushed him to seek professional help and take the steps necessary to reclaim his life.

The Rise to Fame

His rise in popularity after overcoming his battles

After overcoming the battles of addiction and regaining control of his life, Jelly Roll's rise in popularity was both swift and deeply rooted in the authenticity of his story. His music had always resonated with a specific audience, but as he moved forward in his recovery, the raw honesty of his lyrics and the emotional weight behind his songs connected with a much larger group of listeners. People were drawn to the transparency with which he shared his struggles, using his past as a backdrop for his music rather than something to hide from.

Jelly Roll's music was no longer just about pain it was about survival, redemption, and the journey toward healing. This shift in focus brought new depth to his work, and audiences across genres began to take notice. His ability to blend elements of hip-hop with rock and country, while maintaining the emotional authenticity of his storytelling, made him stand out in the music industry. He wasn't confined to one genre, and this crossover appeal opened the doors to a wider fanbase. His music transcended the boundaries of traditional hip-hop, country, and rock, allowing him to connect with listeners from all walks of life.

One of the major turning points in his rise to fame was the release of his collaborations with established artists in both the hip-hop and country music scenes. Songs like "Save Me," which captured the raw emotion of his battle with addiction, showcased Jelly Roll's ability to touch the hearts of his audience while staying true to his gritty, unfiltered style. Tracks like this, which told a story of redemption and hope, resonated with a broad spectrum of fans who had either experienced similar struggles or knew someone who had. His music became anthems for those battling addiction, mental health issues, and personal demons, helping to further solidify his place in the industry.

As his following grew, so did the opportunities to perform on larger stages. From intimate shows in small venues to sold-out concerts at major venues across the country, Jelly Roll's live performances became a critical part of his rise. His shows weren't just about the music they were about connecting with his audience on a deeply personal level. Fans were not only drawn to his powerful voice and storytelling, but also to the vulnerability he brought to the stage. He often spoke openly about his past during performances, further endearing him to his audience and creating a sense of community among those who had been through similar experiences.

Social media and streaming platforms also played a significant role in his rise. Jelly Roll's music found a home online, where fans could easily share and discover his songs. His presence on platforms like YouTube and Spotify helped him reach a global audience, and his down-to-earth, approachable persona resonated with fans who valued authenticity over polished perfection.

Perhaps one of the most significant factors in Jelly Roll's rise after overcoming his battles was his refusal to shy away from his past. Rather than letting his struggles define him in a negative light, he embraced them, using his journey as fuel for his creative fire. This willingness to be vulnerable in his music and in interviews made him a relatable figure, someone who had been through darkness but emerged stronger on the other side. It was this relatability, combined with his undeniable talent, that helped him rise from the underground scene to mainstream recognition.

Key songs and albums that shaped his career
One of the first songs that truly put Jelly Roll on the map was "Pop Another Pill,". Released in 2010, the song exploded in popularity on YouTube, gaining millions of views and giving Jelly Roll his first taste of widespread attention. The track, with its unapologetic lyrics and heavy beats, embodied the raw energy of the Southern hip-hop scene and marked Jelly Roll's rise as a force in underground rap.

As he continued to build his reputation, Jelly Roll's mixtapes began to gain traction. Albums like "Therapeutic Music" and "The Big Sal Story" further showcased his ability to tell deeply personal stories through his lyrics. Therapeutic Music, in particular, revealed the emotional depth of his work, exploring themes of addiction, pain, and survival. The title itself pointed to how important music had become in his healing process.

In 2015, Jelly Roll released "No Filter", a collaborative album with Struggle Jennings, which became another significant milestone in his career. The album combined elements of rap and country, creating a sound that was both hard-hitting and soulful. Songs like "Fall in the Fall" highlighted his evolving musical style, blending hip-hop's raw honesty with country's reflective storytelling. This project marked a turning point for Jelly Roll, as he began to explore more genre-bending sounds, moving beyond pure rap and into new musical territory.

Perhaps the most impactful album in Jelly Roll's career came with "A Beautiful Disaster" in 2020. This album, which included songs like "Save Me" and "Creature," became a defining moment for him. "Save Me," in particular, stood out as one of his most vulnerable and widely acclaimed tracks. With its stripped-down acoustic sound and heartbreaking lyrics about addiction, loneliness, and redemption, the song showed a side of Jelly Roll that fans hadn't seen before. His voice carried a raw emotion that connected with listeners on a deep level, and "Save Me" quickly became an anthem for those struggling with their own demons. The album as a whole allowed Jelly Roll to explore darker, more introspective themes, solidifying his ability to blend hip-hop with rock and country influences.

The follow-up album "Self Medicated" in 2020 continued to build on the momentum Jelly Roll had gained. Songs like "Promise" and "I Need You" further explored his struggles with mental health and addiction, while also showcasing his growth as an artist.

In 2023, Jelly Roll released "Whitsitt Chapel", which marked his full embrace of country music. Named after the church he attended as a child, the album was a reflection of his roots and his journey of redemption.

Songs like "Son of a Sinner" combined country's storytelling tradition with Jelly Roll's own experiences, creating an emotional, introspective body of work that resonated with fans from both the country and hip-hop worlds. The success of "Whitsitt Chapel" on the Billboard charts demonstrated his ability to seamlessly transition between genres while staying true to his personal narrative.

Love, Family, and Personal Life

Insights into his personal relationships and family life

Jelly Roll's personal relationships and family life have been integral to shaping both the man and the artist he is today.

One of the most significant relationships in Jelly Roll's life is with his wife, Bunnie XO (Bunnie DeFord). Bunnie, a podcast host and model, has been a stabilizing force in his life, supporting him through both his career and his personal challenges. Their relationship is built on mutual respect, love, and transparency, and Jelly Roll often speaks about the positive impact she's had on his life. Together, they represent a strong partnership, with Bunnie standing by Jelly Roll through his evolution as a person and artist. Her support has been instrumental in his recovery, offering him a solid foundation of love and encouragement that he had long lacked during the most difficult periods of his life.

Their bond has also become a key part of Jelly Roll's public persona, with the couple often sharing their journey with fans through social media and interviews. They've been open about the challenges they've faced as a couple, but their honesty about the ups and downs has only endeared them more to their fans. Bunnie's unwavering belief in Jelly Roll, especially during times when he doubted himself, has been a cornerstone of their relationship, and her presence in his life has provided him with the stability he needed to turn his life around.

Family extends beyond just his wife Jelly Roll is also a father, and his relationship with his daughter has profoundly impacted his personal growth. Becoming a father gave him a new sense of responsibility and purpose, especially as he worked through his recovery. He often speaks about how the desire to be a good father was one of the driving forces behind his decision to get sober and stay sober. His daughter has been a light in his life, giving him the motivation to rebuild himself and become the man he wanted to be for her. The emotional depth he found in fatherhood has bled into his music, where he often reflects on the importance of family and the pain of being absent during the darker periods of his life.

Jelly Roll's relationship with his family also extends to his broader support network, including friends and fellow artists who have become like family to him. Throughout his career, he has maintained close ties with collaborators like Struggle Jennings and others from the Nashville music scene. These relationships have been forged in both creative and personal growth, with Jelly Roll and his peers sharing similar stories of overcoming adversity. His friends and collaborators have not only supported his musical endeavors but have also been there for him through the personal battles he has faced.

In terms of his extended family, Jelly Roll has openly discussed the difficult dynamics that arose during his years of addiction and legal trouble. His struggles strained relationships with his parents and other relatives, but as he worked through his recovery, he made amends with many of them. The healing process has been slow at times, but rebuilding these relationships has been a priority for Jelly Roll, who values the importance of family despite the difficult history he shares with some of them.

Maintaining balance between fame and personal happiness

For Jelly Roll, maintaining a balance between fame and personal happiness has been a delicate but essential part of his journey. As someone who has experienced both the highs and lows of life ranging from addiction and legal troubles to his eventual rise in the music industry he knows firsthand how fame can complicate the pursuit of inner peace. Yet, his ability to stay grounded, despite growing success, has been a result of conscious effort, the support of his family, and his commitment to staying true to himself.

One of the key ways Jelly Roll has managed to maintain this balance is by keeping his personal life at the forefront of his priorities. While fame has brought new opportunities, it has also presented challenges, such as the constant public scrutiny and the pressures of staying relevant in the music industry. However, Jelly Roll has always made it clear that his family his wife, Bunnie, and his daughter comes first. He understands that without the support of his loved ones, fame would be empty, and personal happiness would be difficult to sustain. His relationship with his wife, in particular, serves as a grounding force. Their bond, built on mutual love and respect, helps him navigate the ups and downs of a demanding career while ensuring that he stays connected to what truly matters.

Fatherhood has also played a major role in how Jelly Roll approaches fame. Being a father has given him a deeper sense of responsibility and purpose, one that extends far beyond the limelight. While the fame might come with its temptations and distractions, Jelly Roll remains focused on being present for his daughter, ensuring that she grows up in a stable and loving environment. This sense of duty has kept him grounded, reminding him that the glitter of fame pales in comparison to the joy of seeing his daughter happy and healthy. He often speaks about how fatherhood has inspired him to stay on track with his recovery and to continue growing as a person, which has had a direct impact on how he manages the pressures of being in the public eye.

Another way Jelly Roll has balanced fame with personal happiness is by maintaining authenticity in both his personal and professional life. Unlike many celebrities who craft a polished, carefully curated public image, Jelly Roll has always been open about his struggles and personal flaws. He doesn't hide behind the facade of fame. Instead, he embraces his imperfections and continues to share his journey with his fans, whether through his music or during interviews. This transparency has allowed him to avoid the common trap of living two separate lives one for the public and one for himself. By staying true to who he is, Jelly Roll has been able to find peace in knowing that his success is built on honesty, not pretense.

Fame has also brought Jelly Roll into the world of larger audiences and constant demands, but he is careful about maintaining a balance between work and personal time. While he dedicates a significant amount of energy to his music career, he makes sure to carve out time for his family and himself, recognizing the importance of stepping away from the pressures of the industry. He often talks about how essential it is to unplug from the noise, spend time with loved ones, and enjoy simple moments outside the fast-paced world of music. This balance is crucial for his mental health and allows him to recharge, so he can continue creating music without burning out.

His commitment to his own mental and emotional well-being has also been a significant factor in maintaining balance. Having struggled with addiction and mental health issues in the past, Jelly Roll knows how easy it is to let external pressures take over. Fame can often bring with it stress, anxiety, and an overwhelming sense of expectation. But for Jelly Roll, self-care is a priority. He actively works on his recovery, attends therapy, and keeps his support system close, ensuring that he doesn't slip back into old patterns. By putting his well-being first, he is able to handle the challenges of fame without sacrificing his personal happiness.

Struggles and Controversies Along the Way

Additional challenges and controversies he faced during his career

Another controversy that has followed Jelly Roll throughout his career is related to his genre-blending approach to music. While many fans appreciate his ability to seamlessly move between hip-hop, country, and rock, some purists in each of these genres have expressed resistance to his style. Critics within the hip-hop community have at times dismissed his country influences, seeing them as a departure from the authenticity of rap. Meanwhile, some country music fans have been skeptical of his hip-hop roots, questioning whether an artist with such a background could truly represent the genre. Despite these criticisms, Jelly Roll has remained unapologetic about his genre-defying sound, asserting that his music is a reflection of his diverse influences and life experiences.

Jelly Roll's physical appearance has also been a point of discussion and, at times, controversy. As a heavily tattooed, larger-than-life figure, he doesn't fit the mold of the typical mainstream artist, and he has faced judgment for it. His tattoos, which cover much of his body, including his face, have led to criticism from those who see them as unprofessional or off-putting. In an industry where image often plays a significant role in success, Jelly Roll's appearance has set him apart but has also made him a target of unfair stereotypes. Rather than conforming to traditional expectations, he has embraced his look as part of his identity, using it to challenge societal norms and demonstrate that talent and heart matter more than appearance.

In addition to these image-related challenges, Jelly Roll has also navigated controversies surrounding some of his collaborations and song content. His work with artists who have faced their own legal and personal issues, such as Struggle Jennings and Lil Wyte, has occasionally drawn criticism from industry insiders who question his choice of collaborators. Moreover, some of his song lyrics, particularly in his early work, have been criticized for their raw and sometimes controversial subject matter, including references to drug use and violence. However, Jelly

Roll has consistently defended his artistic choices, explaining that his music reflects the realities of his life and the world he grew up in.

As his fame has grown, Jelly Roll has also had to grapple with the pressures and controversies that come with being in the public eye. The constant scrutiny from fans and media outlets has put additional pressure on him to maintain a certain image while staying true to himself. He has faced criticism for how he handles his public persona, with some accusing him of capitalizing on his struggles to boost his career. Jelly Roll, however, has consistently stated that his openness about his personal challenges is not a marketing strategy but a way to connect with those who are going through similar hardships. He has made it clear that his music is about telling the truth, no matter how difficult or controversial that truth may be.

Ultimately, the challenges and controversies Jelly Roll has faced during his career have only strengthened his resolve to stay authentic and continue growing as an artist. Each obstacle has forced him to confront his past, defend his creative choices, and stand firm in the face of criticism. His ability to navigate these issues while maintaining his personal integrity has endeared him to a loyal fan base that appreciates his honesty and resilience. While the road hasn't always been smooth, Jelly Roll has turned each challenge into an opportunity for growth, proving that his success is not just about overcoming adversity but embracing it as part of his journey.

How he addressed criticism and challenges publicly

Jelly Roll has faced his share of criticism and challenges throughout his career, but his approach to addressing these issues publicly has been marked by honesty, humility, and a refusal to hide behind a polished image. One of the defining features of his public persona is his willingness to confront criticism head-on, using it as an opportunity for growth and to connect with his audience on a deeper level.

When it comes to the criticism surrounding his personal struggles particularly his battle with addiction

Jelly Roll has always taken an open, transparent stance. Rather than shying away from his troubled past, he frequently talks about his journey through addiction and recovery, acknowledging the mistakes he's made along the way. He doesn't romanticize the challenges he's faced, nor does he paint his recovery as a simple or linear process. Instead, he's honest about the ongoing nature of his struggles, making it clear that sobriety is something he works on every day. His willingness to discuss these issues in such a candid way has not only humanized him but has also endeared him to fans who appreciate his vulnerability.

In response to those who have questioned whether his openness about addiction is genuine, Jelly Roll has consistently emphasized that sharing his story isn't about seeking sympathy or attention. He's made it clear that his goal is to provide hope to others who are battling similar demons, using his music and public platform to inspire those who feel trapped by their circumstances. By being upfront about his struggles and how they've shaped his life and career, he has been able to turn criticism into an opportunity to show that redemption and personal growth are possible, even in the face of adversity.

Legacy

The lasting impact he's had on the music industry

Jelly Roll's lasting impact on the music industry stems from his ability to break down genre barriers, challenge traditional expectations, and connect deeply with his audience through raw, honest storytelling. His career, which began in the underground hip-hop scene and expanded into country and rock, has redefined what it means to be a modern artist. By blending genres that are often seen as distinct or incompatible, Jelly Roll has opened the door for other artists to explore musical diversity without being confined to a single label.

One of the most significant ways Jelly Roll has impacted the music industry is through his genre-blending approach. He seamlessly incorporates elements of hip-hop, country, and rock into his music, demonstrating that artists do not need to fit into a single mold to be successful. His ability to move fluidly between genres has challenged the traditional boundaries of the industry, showing that authenticity and emotional connection matter more than adherence to one style. This shift has encouraged other musicians to explore hybrid sounds, allowing for greater creativity and freedom in an industry that has often been slow to embrace such change. Jelly Roll has proven that an artist can draw from multiple influences and still remain true to their identity, paving the way for a more fluid and inclusive musical landscape.

His storytelling is another area where Jelly Roll has left a lasting mark. His willingness to share deeply personal stories about addiction, mental health, and redemption has resonated with fans who see themselves reflected in his lyrics. Unlike many mainstream artists who rely on catchy hooks or polished personas, Jelly Roll's music is grounded in real-life experiences, making his connection with listeners authentic and meaningful. This level of transparency has shifted how artists approach their music, inspiring others to embrace vulnerability and speak openly about difficult topics. As mental health and addiction continue to be significant challenges in society, Jelly Roll's influence in breaking the stigma around these issues has been profound, encouraging more artists to address similar themes in their work.

Jelly Roll has also impacted how the music industry views success. In an era where viral hits and fleeting fame are often prioritized, he has taken a slower, more organic path to success. His career didn't take off overnight; it was built through years of hard work, consistency, and a loyal fanbase. This approach challenges the industry's often short-sighted focus on instant results and reminds artists and executives alike that long-term success can come from staying true to one's message and steadily building a connection with fans. His rise from underground hip-hop to mainstream recognition shows that authenticity, persistence, and resilience can pay off, even in an industry that tends to favor trends over substance.

Moreover, Jelly Roll has made a significant impact on how the industry embraces artists who don't fit the traditional image of stardom. With his heavily tattooed appearance and unpolished, everyman persona, Jelly Roll defies the stereotypical image of a mainstream music star. Yet, his success proves that talent, honesty, and the ability to connect with an audience are far more important than appearance or adhering to a specific industry mold.

How his music continues to influence new artists and inspire fans

Jelly Roll's music continues to have a profound influence on new artists and inspires fans through its authenticity, emotional depth, and genre-blending style. His ability to speak openly about personal struggles such as addiction, mental health issues, and redemption has created a space for artists and fans alike to explore vulnerability without fear of judgment. This honesty has become a cornerstone of his music, and it's the key reason why his influence extends far beyond his immediate fanbase.

For new artists, Jelly Roll represents a model of how to build a career that's grounded in personal truth rather than commercial trends. His rise from the underground Southern hip-hop scene to mainstream success shows that it is possible to remain authentic while gaining widespread recognition. Young musicians who listen to Jelly Roll see an artist who has defied genre limitations, embracing hip-hop, country, and rock to tell his story in the most genuine way possible. By refusing to conform to the music industry's expectations, Jelly Roll has shown that artistic integrity can be just as important as, if not more than, fitting into a predefined category.

New artists are also drawn to the rawness of his lyrics, which often delve into subjects that are deeply personal and sometimes painful. His openness about his journey through addiction and recovery has made his music a blueprint for artists who want to share their own experiences with mental health, substance abuse, and emotional challenges. Jelly Roll's willingness to lay everything bare has inspired other musicians to be honest in their songwriting, helping to shift the industry toward more authentic and meaningful content. His influence on these emerging artists is evident in how many of them are now more willing to address darker, more personal topics in their music, following Jelly Roll's lead in turning vulnerability into a strength.

Beyond the technical aspects of his music, Jelly Roll's ability to transcend genre boundaries is another way he continues to influence the next generation of artists. By blending hip-hop, country, and rock, Jelly Roll has blurred the lines between genres that traditionally have little overlap. This fluidity has given new artists the confidence to explore different sounds and create music that is not confined to a single genre. His career shows that fans appreciate artists who aren't afraid to experiment and evolve, which has helped open the doors for a more diverse musical landscape. Artists who might have once felt the need to fit into a specific genre are now more inclined to mix influences, following Jelly Roll's example of creative freedom.

For fans, Jelly Roll's music offers not only inspiration but also a sense of connection. His candid lyrics about pain, struggle, and redemption resonate with people who are going through their own battles. Fans frequently credit his music with helping them cope with personal challenges, and many have shared how his songs have provided comfort during their darkest moments. Jelly Roll's ability to channel his personal experiences into his music gives listeners the feeling that they aren't alone and that someone understands what they're going through. His songs are more than just entertainment; they are lifelines for fans who find solace in his message of survival and hope.

The Future of His Career

A look at his current projects and future plans

Currently, Jelly Roll is working on new music that continues to blend his signature mix of emotional storytelling and genre-defying sound. He has hinted at new collaborations with artists across different genres, aiming to further expand his musical horizons. After the success of his album "Whitsitt Chapel" in 2023, which marked his deeper exploration into country music, Jelly Roll is reportedly working on follow-up projects that dive even further into the fusion of country, rock, and hip-hop. Fans can expect more songs that feature the raw, honest lyrics that have become his trademark, with themes that range from personal redemption to reflections on the human condition. Jelly Roll is known for his relentless work ethic in the studio, and it's clear that his creative output isn't slowing down anytime soon.

In addition to releasing new music, Jelly Roll has been focused on performing live and connecting with his fans through tours and concerts. He has built a reputation for his dynamic and emotionally charged live shows, and his future plans include more extensive touring. These performances offer Jelly Roll the chance to engage with his fans on a personal level, something he deeply values. His tours are expected to feature a blend of his older hits, along with new material that showcases his continued musical evolution. As live performances become a key part of his career, Jelly Roll plans to take his shows to new audiences, possibly even expanding into international markets where his fanbase continues to grow.

Jelly Roll is also looking to further his involvement in advocacy work, particularly around mental health awareness and addiction recovery. As someone who has personally battled addiction, Jelly Roll remains committed to using his platform to help others facing similar struggles. He has spoken openly about wanting to increase his efforts in supporting recovery programs and working with organizations that provide mental health resources to underserved communities. His future plans include participating in benefit concerts, partnering with non-profits, and continuing to use his voice to raise awareness around these issues. Jelly Roll's goal is not only to inspire others through his music but also to make a tangible difference in the lives of those affected by addiction and mental health challenges.

Another exciting prospect for Jelly Roll's future is his potential venture into new forms of media. There has been speculation that he may explore opportunities in podcasting or even documentary-style content, where he can delve deeper into his personal story and the stories of others who have faced adversity. Given his openness about his life experiences, a podcast or series where he discusses mental health, addiction, and recovery could offer an intimate look at his journey, as well as provide a platform for other voices to share their stories.

As Jelly Roll continues to grow as an artist, his future plans also include mentoring and collaborating with up-and-coming musicians. He has always been passionate about helping other artists find their voice, particularly those who, like him, come from difficult backgrounds and face significant obstacles. In the future, Jelly Roll may take on a more active role in discovering and supporting new talent, using his experience to guide the next generation of musicians.

Predictions for his ongoing influence in music and beyond

One of the key predictions for Jelly Roll's ongoing influence in music is his continued role in breaking down genre barriers. As an artist who has successfully merged them all, Jelly Roll has already shown that genres are not rigid boundaries but fluid spaces where different styles can coexist. His ability to authentically bridge these worlds has created a new model for artists who don't want to be confined by traditional genre labels. As more emerging musicians seek to experiment with different sounds, Jelly Roll's success will likely inspire them to embrace a similar genre-defying approach. His influence could lead to a broader acceptance of musical hybrids in the industry, encouraging more artists to explore diverse influences without worrying about fitting into a specific mold.

Beyond his impact on genre-blending, Jelly Roll's music will likely continue to influence new generations of artists through its emotional honesty and vulnerability. His willingness to tackle difficult subjects like addiction, mental health struggles, and personal redemption in his lyrics has set a precedent for musicians who want to connect with listeners on a deeper level. As the music industry shifts toward more personal and introspective content, Jelly Roll's ability to turn his pain into art will inspire others to follow suit. In the coming years, we can expect to see more artists embracing transparency in their songwriting, breaking down the barriers between artist and listener, much like Jelly Roll has done.

Jelly Roll's influence will also extend beyond music, particularly in the realms of mental health advocacy and addiction recovery. As someone who has been vocal about his own struggles, Jelly Roll has become a symbol of resilience for many fans who are battling similar issues. His efforts to raise awareness about these topics will likely expand as he continues to use his platform to push for change. In the future, Jelly Roll could play an even bigger role in supporting initiatives that focus on providing resources for addiction recovery and mental health care, particularly in underserved communities. His advocacy work is already making a difference, and as he gains more influence, it's likely that his efforts will inspire broader conversations about these issues in the music industry and beyond.

Jelly Roll's impact will not be limited to his own work; he is poised to become a mentor and role model for other artists who share his background or who face challenges similar to the ones he has overcome. His rise from an underground artist with personal struggles to a mainstream success story will inspire countless others who feel like outsiders in the industry. He has shown that it's possible to find success on your own terms, without compromising who you are or where you come from. This message will resonate with young musicians who are trying to break into the industry, especially those from marginalized or underrepresented communities. As Jelly Roll continues to collaborate with and mentor up-and-coming artists, his influence will extend to shaping the careers of future stars who look up to him for guidance and inspiration.

In terms of his cultural impact, Jelly Roll's commitment to his fanbase and his community will continue to play a significant role in his ongoing influence. He has always maintained a strong connection with his fans, not just through his music but through personal interactions and engagement on social media. This close relationship with his audience will ensure that his message of resilience and hope continues to spread. His influence will likely grow as more people discover his music and relate to the authenticity of his journey, creating a community of listeners who feel empowered by his story.

As Jelly Roll's platform continues to expand, it's possible that his influence could even move beyond music into other forms of media or public advocacy. He has already shown interest in using his voice to effect social change, and in the future, we might see him take on more prominent roles in charitable efforts or even in producing content that raises awareness about addiction, mental health, and other social issues. His potential to influence conversations in these areas will only increase as his career progresses, making him a key figure not just in music but in broader cultural discussions about resilience, recovery, and personal growth.

The Power of Redemption and Music

Recap of his journey from struggle to success

Jelly Roll's journey from struggle to success is a story of resilience, redemption, and the power of authenticity. Born Jason Bradley DeFord in Nashville, Tennessee, Jelly Roll grew up in a tough environment, surrounded by poverty, addiction, and instability. From an early age, he found himself entangled in trouble, facing legal issues and battling a deep struggle with addiction that threatened to derail his life. These early years were marked by a sense of isolation and pain, as he navigated through the consequences of his choices while struggling to find a way out.

Music became Jelly Roll's lifeline, offering him an outlet for the pain and frustration he felt. He first turned to hip-hop, where he found a way to express the realities of his life through raw, unfiltered lyrics. His early tracks, filled with stories of addiction, crime, and personal battles, resonated with listeners in Nashville's underground hip-hop scene. His collaboration with Lil Wyte on the 2010 track "Pop Another Pill" was a turning point, gaining millions of views and putting

Jelly Roll on the map. However, despite this success, his personal struggles with addiction continued to weigh heavily on him, threatening to overshadow his growing musical career.

Jelly Roll's journey toward recovery wasn't immediate. He faced years of relapses and setbacks as he fought to break free from the cycle of addiction. His legal troubles, combined with the emotional toll of his battles, made it difficult for him to maintain stability in both his personal life and his career. But through it all, music remained a constant a way for him to process his pain and share his story. It was through his music that he began to find a path toward healing, using his songs to reflect not just the darkness he experienced, but the possibility of redemption.

As Jelly Roll began to overcome his personal demons, his music evolved as well. He expanded beyond hip-hop, embracing elements of country and rock, genres that had always influenced him growing up in Nashville. This blending of styles allowed him to reach new audiences, and his ability to fuse these genres with deeply personal storytelling set him apart from other artists. Albums like "A Beautiful Disaster" and "Self Medicated" were pivotal in showcasing his emotional depth and his willingness to confront his past openly and honestly. Songs like "Save Me" became anthems for those struggling with addiction and mental health issues, as Jelly Roll used his platform to share the lessons he had learned through his own journey.

Jelly Roll's rise to mainstream success came as he fully embraced his role as a genre-defying artist. With the release of "Whitsitt Chapel" in 2023, he solidified his place in the country music scene while maintaining the authenticity that had always been at the core of his music. The album's success, particularly the track "Son of a Sinner," reflected the power of his storytelling and his ability to connect with fans across different musical backgrounds. His concerts became emotional experiences, where fans felt a deep connection to his music and his message of resilience.

But Jelly Roll's success isn't just measured in albums or chart placements. His journey is one of personal transformation, from a man caught in the grips of addiction and legal troubles to an artist who uses his platform to inspire and support others. He has become a powerful advocate for mental health awareness and addiction recovery, speaking openly about his struggles and encouraging others to seek help. His efforts to give back to his community and raise awareness about these issues have made him not just a successful musician, but a symbol of hope for those facing similar battles.

The lasting message of hope and perseverance
Jelly Roll's lasting message of hope and perseverance is one that resonates deeply with his fans and reflects the core of his life and music. His journey from addiction, legal troubles, and personal despair to success and personal redemption serves as a powerful reminder that no matter how dark life may seem, there is always a path to healing and transformation. His story is one of resilience of falling, getting back up, and refusing to let past mistakes define the future.

At the heart of Jelly Roll's message is the idea that change is possible, even for those who feel trapped by their circumstances. Through his music, he offers a raw and honest portrayal of his struggles, openly sharing his experiences with addiction, mental health issues, and the pain of feeling lost. His willingness to confront these issues head-on has made him a relatable figure to many who are going through similar battles. He shows that no matter how deep the pain, there is always a way to rise above it. By turning his darkest moments into a source of strength, Jelly Roll encourages his listeners to believe that they, too, can overcome the obstacles in their lives.

Perseverance is another key theme in Jelly Roll's message. His rise to success wasn't quick or easy it was the result of years of hard work, personal reflection, and a relentless determination to move forward. He acknowledges that the road to recovery, whether from addiction, emotional trauma, or life's challenges, is often filled with setbacks. However, he emphasizes that the important thing is to keep going, even when it feels impossible. Through his own journey, he has shown that perseverance can lead to transformation, and that success is not defined by never falling, but by getting up every time you do.

Jelly Roll's music serves as a lifeline for many, offering messages of survival, self-acceptance, and growth. His songs are filled with stories of people who are struggling but still fighting, and this resonates with listeners who may feel isolated in their own battles. His music tells them that they are not alone and that their struggles do not make them weak. Instead, they are part of the human experience, and it is through facing these challenges that we find strength. The hope Jelly Roll provides is not about perfection or a flawless journey, but about the possibility of redemption and the belief that no one is beyond saving.

In addition to his personal story, Jelly Roll uses his platform to advocate for mental health awareness and addiction recovery, further reinforcing his message of hope. He encourages people to seek help, reminding them that there is no shame in asking for support and that recovery is an ongoing process. His openness about his own struggles helps to break down the stigma that often surrounds these issues, offering hope to those who might otherwise feel too afraid to take the first step toward healing.

Ultimately, Jelly Roll's message of hope and perseverance is about finding light in the darkest moments. It's about understanding that setbacks are part of the journey, but they do not define who you are or what you're capable of achieving. His music and his life serve as a powerful example that even when everything feels hopeless, there is always the possibility for a better tomorrow. By sharing his story so openly, Jelly Roll gives his fans not only a soundtrack to their struggles but also the inspiration to keep pushing forward, no matter how hard the road may seem.

Through his honesty, resilience, and unwavering belief in the power of transformation, Jelly Roll's message of hope and perseverance will continue to inspire those who listen to his music and follow his journey. It's a reminder that no matter how many times life knocks you down, it's always possible to get back up and keep moving forward.

Made in United States
North Haven, CT
22 November 2024